THIS BOOK IS LITERALLY JUST PICTURES OF ANIMALS SILENTLY JUDGING YOU

Smith
Street
Books

Smith Street Books

Published in 2021 by Smith Street Books
Naarm | Melbourne | Australia
smithstreetbooks.com

ISBN: 9781922417046

Publisher: Paul McNally
Design and layout: Hannah Koelmeyer
Picture research: Avery Hayes
Cover photo: Karsten Winegeart/Unsplash

Printed & bound in China by C&C Offset Printing Co., Ltd.

Book 155
10 9 8 7 6 5 4